—

THE ILLUMINATED
Christmas Songbook

THE ILLUMINATED
Christmas Songbook

Turner Publishing, Inc.

ATLANTA

Published by Turner Publishing, Inc.
A Subsidiary of Turner Broadcasting System, Inc.
1050 Techwood Drive, N.W.
Atlanta, Georgia 30318

Distributed to the trade by Andrews and McMeel
A Universal Press Syndicate Company
4520 Main Street
Kansas City, Missouri 64111

Published in cooperation with and distributed to the religious market by
Oxford University Press, Inc.
198 Madison Avenue
New York, New York 10016

First Edition 10 9 8 7 6 5 4 3 2 1

ISBN: 1-57036-370-6

Cover Design: Michael J. Walsh; Book Design: Karen E. Smith; Photo Editor: Marty Moore;
Editors: Walton Rawls and Michon Wise; Production: Caroline Reaves

Printed in the United States

A Christmas Song Treasury for the

_____

Family

Given on

_____

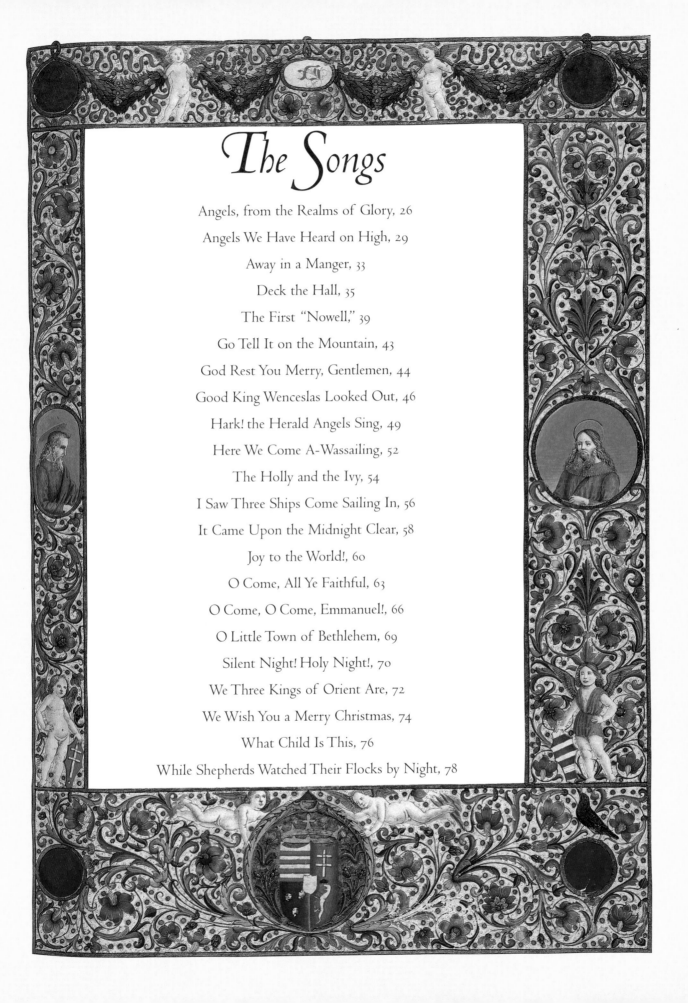

The Songs

Make a joyful noise unto the Lord . . .

Psalm 98: 4

The Christmas Story

*I*n the sixth month the angel Gabriel was sent by God to a town in Galilee called Nazareth, to a virgin engaged to a man whose name was Joseph, of the house of David. The virgin's name was Mary. And he came to her and said, "Greetings, favored one! The Lord is with you." But she was much perplexed by his words and pondered what sort of greeting this might be. The angel said to her, "Do not be afraid, Mary, for you have found favor with God. And now, you will conceive in your womb and bear a son, and you will name him Jesus."

Luke 1: 26-31

*I*n those days a decree went out from Emperor Augustus that all the world should be registered. This was the first registration and was taken while Quirinius was governor of Syria. All went to their own towns to be registered. Joseph also went from the town of Nazareth in Galilee to Judea, to the city of David called Bethlehem, because he was descended from the house and family of David. He went to be registered with Mary, to whom he was engaged and who was expecting a child. While they were there, the time came for her to deliver her child. And she gave birth to her firstborn son and wrapped him in bands of cloth, and laid him in a manger, because there was no place for them in the inn.

Luke 2: 1-7

*I*n that region there were shepherds living in the fields, keeping watch over their flock by night. Then an angel of the Lord stood before them, and the glory of the Lord shone around them, and they were terrified. But the angel said to them, "Do not be afraid; for see—I am bringing you good news of great joy for all the people: to you is born this day in the city of David a Savior, who is the Messiah, the Lord. This will be a sign for you: you will find a child wrapped in bands of cloth and lying in a manger."

Luke 2: 8-12

*I*n the time of King Herod, after Jesus was born in Bethlehem of Judea, wise men from the East came to Jerusalem, asking, "Where is the child who has been born king of the Jews? For we observed his star at its rising, and have come to pay him homage." When King Herod heard this, he was frightened, and all Jerusalem with him. . . . Then Herod secretly called for the wise men and learned from them the exact time when the star had appeared. . . . When they had heard the king, they set out; and there, ahead of them, went the star that they had seen at its rising, until it stopped over the place where the child was. When they saw that the star had stopped, they were overwhelmed with joy. On entering the house, they saw the child with Mary his mother; and they knelt down and paid him homage. Then, opening their treasure chests, they offered him gifts of gold, frankincense, and myrrh.

Matthew 2: 1-3, 7, 9-11

After eight days had passed, it was time to circumcise the child; and he was called Jesus, the name given by the angel before he was conceived in the womb. When the time came for their purification according to the law of Moses, they brought him up to Jerusalem to present him to the Lord (as it is written in the law of the Lord, "Every firstborn male shall be designated as holy to the Lord"), and they offered a sacrifice according to what is stated in the law of the Lord, "a pair of turtledoves or two young pigeons."

Luke 2: 21-24

Now after they had left, an angel of the Lord appeared to Joseph in a dream and said, "Get up, take the child and his mother, and flee to Egypt, and remain there until I tell you; for Herod is about to search for the child, to destroy him." Then Joseph got up, took the child and his mother by night, and went to Egypt, and remained there until the death of Herod. This was to fulfill what had been spoken by the Lord through the prophet, "Out of Egypt I have called my son."

Matthew 2: 13-15

The Songs

Angels, from the Realms of Glory

James Montgomery (1771–1854)

Henry Smart (1813–79)

1. An - gels, from the realms of glo - ry, Wing your flight o'er all the earth;
Ye who sang Cre - a - tion's sto - ry Now pro - claim Mes - si - ah's birth!

Refrain

Come and wor - ship, come and wor - ship, wor - ship Christ the___ new - born King!

2. Shepherds, in the field abiding,
   Watching o'er your flocks by night:
   God with man is now residing,
   Yonder shines the Infant Light.

3. Sages, leave your contemplations:
   Brighter visions beam afar.
   Seek the Great Desire of Nations:
   Ye have seen his natal star.

4. Saints, before the altar bending,
   Watching long in hope and fear:
   Suddenly the Lord, descending,
   In his temple shall appear.

5. Though an infant now we view him,
   He shall fill his Father's throne,
   Gather all the nations to him;
   Every knee shall then bow down.

Angels We Have Heard on High

Angels We Have Heard on High

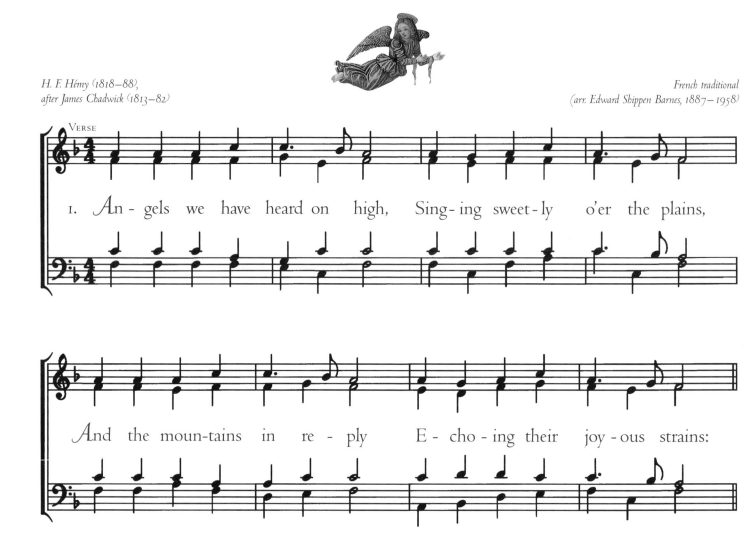

H. F. Hémy (1818–88),
after James Chadwick (1813–82)

French traditional
(arr. Edward Shippen Barnes, 1887–1958)

VERSE

1. An-gels we have heard on high, Sing-ing sweet-ly o'er the plains,

And the moun-tains in re - ply E - cho - ing their joy - ous strains:

2. Shepherds, why this jubilee?
    Why these joyous strains prolong?
  What the gladsome tidings be
    Which inspire your heavenly song?

3. Come to Bethlehem and see
    Him whose birth the angels sing;
  Come, adore on bended knee
    Christ the Lord, the newborn King!

4. See him in a manger laid,
    Whom the choirs of angels praise;
  Mary, Joseph, lend your aid,
    While our hearts in love we raise.

Away in a Manger

Anon. (Murray, 1887)   James R. Murray (1841/2–1905)

1. A - way in a man - ger, no crib for a bed, The_ lit - tle Lord

Je - sus laid_ down his sweet head; The stars in the sky_____ looked

down where he lay__ The lit - tle Lord Je - sus, a - sleep on the hay.

2. The cattle are lowing, the Baby awakes,
   But little Lord Jesus, no crying he makes.
   I love thee, Lord Jesus! look down from the sky,
   And stay by my cradle till morning is nigh.

3. Be near me, Lord Jesus: I ask thee to stay
   Close by me forever, and love me, I pray;
   Bless all the dear children in thy tender care,
   And take us to heaven to live with thee there.

Deck the Hall
with
Boughs of Holly

Deck the Hall with Boughs of Holly

Anon.

Welsh traditional
(Jones, 1784, arr. Hugh Keyte and Andrew Parrott.
Copyright Oxford University Press. All rights reserved.)

1. Deck the hall with boughs of hol - ly: Fal, la, la, la, la,_____ la, la, la!

'Tis the sea - son to be jol - ly! Fal, la, la, la, la,_____ la, la, la!

Don we now our gay ap-par-el, Fal, la, la, la, la, la,____ la, la, la!

Troll the an-cient Yule-tide ca-rol. Fal, la, la, la, la,____ la, la, la!

2. See the blazing yule before us!
   Strike the harp and join the chorus!
   Follow me in merry measure,
   While I tell of Yuletide treasure.

3. Fast away the old year passes,
   Hail the new, ye lads and lasses!
   Sing we joyous, all together,
   Heedless of the wind and weather.

The First "Nowell"

The First "Nowell"

Sandys, 1833, adapted

English traditional (Sandys, 1833,
arr. John Stainer, 1840–1901)

REFRAIN

was _____ so deep. No - well! _____ no - well! no - well! _____ no -

~ well! _____ Born is the King _____ of Is ~ ra ~ el!

2. They lookèd up and saw a star
   Shining in the east, beyond them far;
   And to the earth it gave great light,
   And so continued both day and night.

3. And by the light of that same star
   Three wise men came from country far;
   To seek for a King was their intent,
   And to follow the star wheresoever it went.

4. This star drew nigh to the northwest:
   O'er Bethlehem it took its rest;
   And there it did both stop and stay,
   Right over the place where Jesus lay.

5. Then entered in those wise men three,
   Full reverently, upon their knee,
   And offered there, in his presence,
   Both gold and myrrh, and frankincense.

6. Then let us all with one accord
   Sing praises to our heavenly Lord
   That hath made heaven and earth of nought,
   And with his blood mankind hath bought.

Go Tell It on the Mountain

American traditional
(Thomas P. Fenner, 1909, arr. Hugh Keyte and Andrew Parrott.
Copyright Oxford University Press. All rights reserved.)

1. In the time of Da - vid,_____ Some call him a king, And if a child is true - born, Lord Je - sus will hear him sing:____

Go tell it on the moun - tain, O - ver the hills and e - ve - ry-where;

Go tell it on the moun - tain That Je - sus Christ____ is born!

2. When I was a seeker
   I sought both night and day;
   I ask the Lord to help me,
   And he show me the way.

3. He made me a watchman
   Upon a city wall,
   And if I am a Christian
   I am the least of all.

God Rest You Merry, Gentlemen

West Country traditional
(Sandys, 1833)

English traditional
(arr. John Stainer, 1840—1901)

VERSE

1. God rest you mer-ry, gen-tle-men, Let no-thing you dis - may, For

Je - sus Christ, our Sa - vior, Was born up - on this

day To save us all from Sa - tan's power When we were gone a -

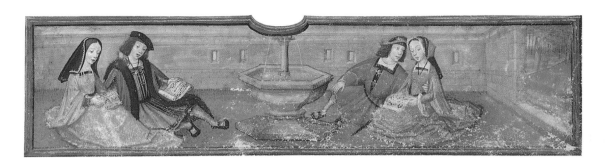

-stray.___ O___ ti - dings of com ~ fort and joy, com-fort and joy,___ O___ ti - dings of com ~ fort and joy!

2. *I*n Bethlehem in Jewry
   This blessèd Babe was born,
And laid within a manger
   Upon this blessèd morn;
The which his mother Mary
   Nothing did take in scorn.

3. *F*rom God our heavenly Father
   A blessèd angel came,
And unto certain shepherds
   Brought tidings of the same,
How that in Bethlehem was born
   The Son of God by name.

4. *"F*ear not," then said the angel,
   "Let nothing you affright;
This day is born a Savior
   Of virtue, power and might,
So frequently to vanquish all
   The friends of Satan quite."

5. *T*he shepherds at those tidings
   Rejoicèd much in mind,
And left their flocks a-feeding
   In tempest, storm and wind,
And went to Bethlehem straightway
   This blessèd Babe to find.

6. *B*ut when to Bethlehem they came,
   Whereat this Infant lay,
They found him in a manger,
   Where oxen feed on hay;
His mother Mary, kneeling,
   Unto the Lord did pray.

7. *N*ow to the Lord sing praises,
   All you within this place,
And with true love and brotherhood
   Each other now embrace.
The holy tide of Christmas
   All others doth efface.

Good King Wenceslas Looked Out

J. M. Neale (1818–66)

Fourteenth-century Piae Cantiones (1582)
(arr. John Stainer, 1840–1901)

1. Good King Wen - ces - las looked out On the feast of Ste - phen,
When the snow lay round a - bout, Deep and crisp and e - ven;

Bright - ly shone the moon that night, Though the frost was cru - el,

When a poor man came in sight, Gath-'ring win - ter fu - el.

2. "Hither, page and stand by me;
   If thou know'st it, telling—
   Yonder peasant, who is he?
   Where and what his dwelling?"
   "Sire, he lives a good league hence,
   Underneath the mountain,
   Right against the forest fence,
   By Saint Agnes' fountain."

3. "Bring me flesh, and bring me wine!
   Bring me pine logs hither!
   Thou and I will see him dine
   When we bear them thither."
   Page and monarch forth they went,
   Forth they went together,
   Through the rude wind's wild lament
   And the bitter weather.

4. "Sire, the night is darker now,
   And the wind blows stronger;
   Fails my heart, I know not how,
   I can go no longer."
   "Mark my footsteps, good my page,
   Tread thou in them boldly:
   Thou shalt find the winter's rage
   Freeze thy blood less coldly."

5. In his master's steps he trod,
   Where the snow lay dinted;
   Heat was in the very sod
   Which the saint had printed.
   Therefore, Christian men, be sure,
   Wealth or rank possessing,
   Ye who now will bless the poor
   Shall yourselves find blessing.

Hark! the Herald Angels Sing

Hark! the Herald Angels Sing

Charles Wesley (1707–88) and others

"C. B." (Martin Madan, 1769)

1. Hark! hark the he-rald_ an-gels_ sing: "Glo - ry

to_____ the new-born_ King!_ Peace on earth and mer - cy

mild,_ God and_ sin - ners re - con - ciled!"

Joy - ful,__ all ye____ na - tions, rise! Join the__

tri-umphs of___ the_ skies! With th'an - gel - ic host___ pro -

SOLI

- claim: "Christ is___ born in___ Beth-le - hem!_ Christ is born_____

FULL   SOLI

_____ in Beth-le - hem!" Hark!__ the he - rald an - gels__ sing:__

FULL

"Glo-ry__ to__ the_new-born King!"

ORGAN

2. Hail! hail the heav'n born Prince of Peace!   Ris'n with healing in his wings.   Born to raise the sons of earth,
   Hail the Sun of Righteousness!   Mild, he lays his glory by,   Born to give them second birth,
   Light and life to all he brings,   Born that man no more may die,   born to give them second birth.

51

Here We Come A-Wassailing

W. H. Husk, 1864

English traditional
(Bramley and Stainer, 1871, arr. Hugh Keyte and Andrew Parrott.
Copyright Oxford University Press. All rights reserved.)

1. Here we come a - was - sail - ing A - mong the leaves so green;____ Here we come a - wan - der - ing, So fair____ to be seen. Love and joy come to you, And to you your was - sail too, And God bless you, and send____ you a hap - py new year, And God send you a hap - py new year.

2. Our wassail cup is made
    Of the rosemary tree,
And so is your beer
    Of the best barley.

3. We are not daily beggars
    That beg from door to door,
But we are neighbors' children
    Whom you have seen before.

4. Call up the butler of this house,
    Put on his golden ring;
Let him bring us up a glass of beer,
    And better we shall sing.

5. We have got a little purse
    Of stretching leather skin;
We want a little of your money
    To line it well within.

6. Bring us out a table,
    And spread it with a cloth;
Bring us out some moldy cheese,
    And some of your Christmas loaf.

7. God bless the master of this house,
    Likewise the mistress too,
And all the little children
    That round the table go.

8. Good master and good mistress,
    While you're sitting by the fire,
Pray think of us poor children
    Who are wandering in the mire.

The Holly and the Ivy

English traditional
(Sharp, 1911, arr. Hugh Keyte and Andrew Parrott.
Copyright Oxford University Press. All rights reserved.)

Sharp, 1911

VERSE
SOLO/SOLI

1. The hol-ly and the i - vy, When they are both full grown, Of___
all the trees that are in the wood, The__ hol-ly bears the crown.

2. The holly bears a blossom
   As white as the lily flower,
   And Mary bore sweet Jesus Christ
   To be our sweet Savior.

3. The holly bears a berry
   As red as any blood,
   And Mary bore sweet Jesus Christ
   To do poor sinners good.

4. The holly bears a prickle
   As sharp as any thorn,
   And Mary bore sweet Jesus Christ
   On Christmas Day in the morn.

The ri - sing of the___ sun___ And the run - ning of___ the___

deer,___ The___ play-ing of the mer-ry or - gan, Sweet sing-ing in___ the choir.

5. The holly bears a bark
   As bitter as any gall,
   And Mary bore sweet Jesus Christ
   For to redeem us all.

6. The holly and the ivy,
   When they are both full grown,
   Of all the trees that are in the wood,
   The holly bears the crown.

I Saw Three Ships Come Sailing In

Sandys, 1833

English traditional
(Bramley and Stainer, c. 1878, arr. Hugh Keyte and Andrew Parrott.
Copyright Oxford University Press. All rights reserved.)

1. I saw three ships come sail-ing in On Christ - mas Day, on Christ - mas Day, I saw three ships come sail - ing in On Christ - mas Day in the morn - ing.

2. And what was in those ships all three?

3. Our Savior Christ and his lady,

4. Pray, whither sailed those ships all three?

5. O they sailed into Bethlehem

6. And all the bells on earth shall ring

7. And all the angels in heaven shall sing

8. And all the souls on earth shall sing

9. Then let us all rejoice amain!

It Came Upon the Midnight Clear

Edmund H. Sears (1810–76)

Richard Storrs Willis (1819–1900)
(arr. Uzziah Christopher Burnap, 1834–1900)

1. It came up-on__ the mid-night clear, That glo - rious song_ of old,____ From an - gels, bend - ing near the earth To touch their harps of gold:____ "Peace on the earth, good-will to men From heaven's all - gra - cious King!"__ The world in so - lemn still - ness lay To hear the an - gels sing.___

2. Still through the cloven skies they come,
   With peaceful wings unfurled,
   And still their heavenly music floats
   O'er all the weary world:
   Above its sad and lowly plains
   They bend on hovering wing,
   And ever o'er its Babel sounds
   The blessèd angels sing.

3. Yet with the woes of sin and strife
   The world has suffered long:
   Beneath the angels' strain have rolled
   Two thousand years of wrong,
   And man, at war with man, hears not
   The love-song which they bring:
   O hush the noise, ye men of strife,
   And hear the angels sing!

4. And ye, beneath life's crushing load,
   Whose forms are bending low,
   Who toil along the climbing way
   With painful steps and slow,
   Look now! for glad and golden hours
   Come swiftly on the wing;
   O rest beside the weary road,
   And hear the angels sing!

5. For lo! the days are hastening on,
   By prophet-bards foretold,
   When, with the ever-circling years,
   Comes round the Age of Gold,
   When peace shall over all the earth
   Its ancient splendors fling,
   And the whole world give back the song
   Which now the angels sing.

Joy to the World!

Isaac Watts (1674–1748)

Pre-1833
(rev. William Holford, c. 1834, arr. Hugh Keyte and Andrew Parrott.
Copyright Oxford University Press. All rights reserved.)

1. Joy to____ the world!____ the__ Lord is come: Let

earth re - ceive____ her King!_____ Let

ev - 'ry____ heart____ pre - pare____ him____ room,____

And heav'n and na-ture sing, and heav'n and na-ture sing, and

1.
(Repeat ad lib.)

2.

heav'n,____ and heav'n____ and na - ture sing! sing!

2. *J*oy to the earth! the Savior reigns:
   Let men their songs employ,
   While fields and floods, rocks, hills, and plains
   Repeat the sounding joy.

3. *H*e rules the world with truth and grace,
   And makes the nations prove
   The glories of his righteousness
   And wonders of his love.

O Come, All Ye Faithful

O Come, All Ye Faithful

Frederick Oakeley (1802–80), adapted

Anon. (An Essay on the Church Plain Chant, 1782,
arr. Thomas Greatorex, 1757–1831, adapted)

1. O come, all ye faith-ful, Joy-ful and tri-um-phant, O come ye, O come ye to Beth-le-hem! Come and be-hold him, Born the King of An-gels! O come, let us a-dore him! O come, let us a-dore him! O come, let us a-dore____ him, Christ_ the Lord!

Come and be - hold him, Born the King of An - gels! O come, let us a - dore him! O

come, let us a - dore him! O come, let us a - dore_____ him, Christ____ the Lord!

2. Sing, choirs of angels!
   Sing in exultation!
   Sing, all ye citizens of heaven above:
   "Glory to God
   In the highest."

3. Yea, Lord, we greet thee,
   Born this happy morning;
   Jesu, to thee be glory given,
   Word of the Father
   Now in flesh appearing.

O Come, O Come, Emmanuel!

tr. J. M. Neale (1818—66)
rev. T. A. Lacey (1853—1931), adapted

Thirteenth century?
(Bibliothèque Nationale MS, arr. Hugh Keyte and Andrew Parrott.

VERSE

1. O come, O come, Em - ma - nu - el! And ran - som cap - tive
Is - ra - el That mourns in lone - ly exile_____ here, Un -

REFRAIN

- til the Son of God_____ ap - pear. Re - joice! re - joice! Em -

-ma - nu -el Shall come to thee, O Is - ra - el.

2. *O* come, thou Branch of Jesse! Draw
   The quarry from the lion's claw;
   From the dread caverns of the grave,
   From nether hell, thy people save.

3. *O* come, O come, thou Dayspring bright!
   Pour on our souls thy healing light;
   Dispel the long night's lingering gloom,
   And pierce the shadows of the tomb.

4. *O* come, thou Key of David, come,
   And open wide our heavenly home;
   Safeguard for us the heavenward road,
   And bar the way to death's abode.

5. *O* come, O come, Adonaï,
   Who in thy glorious majesty
   From Sinai's mountain, clothed in awe,
   Gavest thy folk the elder Law.

Eus madiutorium
meum intende.
Domine ad adiu
uandum me festina

O Little Town of Bethlehem

Phillips Brooks (1835–93)

Lewis H. Redner (1831–1908)

1. O lit-tle town of Beth-le-hem, How still we_ see thee lie! A-bove thy deep and dream-less sleep The si-lent stars go by. Yet in thy dark streets shi-neth The e-ver-last-ing Light: The hopes and fears of all the years Are_ met in_ thee to-night.

2. O morning stars, together
  Proclaim the holy Birth!
And praises sing to God the King,
  And peace to men on earth;
For Christ is born of Mary,
  And, gathered all above,
While mortals sleep, the angels keep
  Their watch of wondering love.

3. How silently, how silently
  The wondrous gift is given!
So God imparts to human hearts
  The blessings of his heaven.
No ear may hear his coming,
  But, in this world of sin,
Where meek souls will receive him, still
  The dear Christ enters in.

4. Where children pure and happy
  Pray to the blessèd Child;
Where misery cries out to thee,
  Son of the mother mild;
Where Charity stands watching
  And Faith holds wide the door,
The dark night wakes, the glory breaks,
  And Christmas comes once more.

5. O holy child of Bethlehem,
  Descend to us we pray;
Cast out our sin, and enter in:
  Be born to us today!
We hear the Christmas angels
  The great glad tidings tell;
O come to us, abide with us,
  Our Lord Emmanuel!

Silent Night! Holy Night!

tr. John F. Young, 1820–85

Modern version
after Franz Xaver Gruber (1787–1863) (arr. Hugh Keyte and
Andrew Parrott. Copyright Oxford University Press. All rights reserved.)

1. Si - lent night! ho - ly night! All is calm, all is bright

Round yon Vir - gin Mo-ther and Child; Ho - ly In-fant so ten-der and mild,

Sleep in hea - ven-ly peace!___ Sleep_ in hea - ven-ly peace!

2. *Silent night! holy night!*
   Shepherds quake at the sight;
   Glories stream from heaven afar,
   Heavenly hosts sing: "Alleluia!
   Christ the Savior is born!
   Christ the Savior is born!"

3. *Silent night! holy night!*
   Son of God, love's pure light,
   Radiant, beams from thy holy face
   With the dawn of redeeming grace,
   Jesus, Lord, at thy birth!
   Jesus, Lord, at thy birth!

We Three Kings of Orient Are

Words and music by John Henry Hopkins (1820–91)

VERSE

1. We three kings of O - ri - ent are, Bearing gifts we tra - verse a -far, Field and foun-tain, moor and moun-tain, Fol-low-ing yon - der star.

REFRAIN

O____ Star of Won ~ der, Star of Night, Star with roy - al beau -ty bright,

West - ward lead ~ ing, still pro -ceed ~ ing, Guide us to thy per - fect light.

2. Born a king on Bethlehem plain,
   Gold I bring to crown him again,
   King for ever, ceasing never
   Over us all to reign.

3. Frankincense to offer have I,
   Incense owns a Deity nigh;
   Prayer and praising all men raising,
   Worship him, God on high.

4. Myrrh is mine; its bitter perfume
   Breathes a life of gathering gloom;
   Sorrowing, sighing, bleeding, dying,
   Sealed in the stone-cold tomb.

5. Glorious now behold him arise,
   King, and God, and sacrifice.
   Heaven sing: "Alleluia";
   "Alleluia" the earth replies.

We Wish You a Merry Christmas

English traditional (arr. Hugh Keyte and Andrew Parrott.
Copyright Oxford University Press. All rights reserved.)

1. We wish you a mer-ry Christ-mas, we wish you a mer-ry

Christ-mas, we wish you a mer-ry Christ-mas and a hap-py new year!

Glad_ ti - dings we__ bring To you and your kin: We

wish you a mer ~ ry Christ - mas__ And a hap - py__ new year!

2. *N*ow bring us some figgy pudding,
Now bring us some figgy pudding,
Now bring us some figgy pudding,
And bring it us here!

3. *O* we won't go until we've got some,
No, we won't go until we've got some,
We won't go until we've got some,
So give it us here!

4. *O* we all like figgy pudding,
Yes, we all like figgy pudding,
We all like figgy pudding,
So bring it out here!

What Child Is This

William Chatterton Dix (1837–98)

Traditional
(arr. John Stainer, 1840–1901)

1. What child is this__ who, laid to rest,__ On Ma-ry's lap___ is sleep-ing, Whom

an-gels greet_ with an-thems sweet While shep-herds watch_ are keep-ing?

This, this__ is Christ the King, Whom shep-herds guard_ and an-gels sing:

Haste, haste__ to bring him laud,_ The Babe,__ the Son___ of Ma-ry!

2. Why lies he in such mean estate
   Where ox and ass are feeding?
   Good Christians fear: for sinners here
   The silent Word is pleading.
   Nail, spear shall pierce him through,
   The Cross be borne for me, for you;
   Hail! hail the Word Made Flesh,
   The Babe, the Son of Mary!

3. So bring him incense, gold and myrrh;
   Come, peasant, king, to own him!
   The King of Kings salvation brings:
   Let loving hearts enthrone him!
   Raise, raise the song on high!
   The Virgin sings her lullaby.
   Joy! joy! for Christ is born,
   The Babe, the Son of Mary!

While Shepherds Watched Their Flocks By Night

Nahum Tate? (1652–1715)   *after George Frideric Handel (1685–1759)*

2. "Fear not," said he (for mighty dread
   Had seized their troubled mind),
   "Glad tidings of great joy I bring
   To you and all mankind.

3. "To you in David's town this day
   Is born of David's line
   The Savior, who is Christ the Lord;
   And this shall be the sign:

4. "The heavenly Babe you there shall find
   To human view displayed,
   All meanly wrapped in swathing bands,
   And in a manger laid."

5. Thus spake the seraph; and forthwith
   Appeared a shining throng
   Of angels, praising God, who thus
   Addressed their joyful song:

6. "All glory be to God on high,
   And to the earth be peace;
   Good will henceforth from heaven to men
   Begin and never cease."

Illustrations

All illustrations in *The Illuminated Christmas Songbook* are taken from the Latin manuscript collections of The Vatican Library. They are traditionally identified as coming from a certain collection by manuscript number and folio, recto or verso. Hence, the citation "Urb. Lat. 2 folio 239 r" stands for folio 239 recto in Latin manuscript 2 in the Urbino Collection of The Vatican Library. The full names of other collections cited in abbreviated fashion are Barberini, Borghese, Capponi, Chigi, Ottoboni, Reginense, and Vatican.

Front cover, opening page: Urb. Lat. 2 folio 239 r; frontispiece: Chigi CVIII 234 folio 3 v; copyright page: Vat. Lat. 3770 folio 200 r; dedication page: Reg. Lat. 128 folio 53 v; table of contents: Urb. Lat. 112 folio 357 v; p. 11: Urb. Lat. 2; pp. 12, 13: Vat. Lat. 3781 folio 23 r; pp. 14, 15: Vat. Lat. 3781 folio 37 v; pp. 16, 17: Vat. Lat. 3781 folio 40 v; pp. 18, 19: Vat. Lat. 3781 folio 43 r; pp. 20, 21: Vat. Lat. 3781 folio 45 v; pp. 22, 23: Vat. Lat. 3781 folio 48 r; p. 25: Barb. Lat. 613 folio 314 v; p. 27: Vat. Lat. 3770 folio 148 v; pp. 28, 29: Vat. Lat. 3770 folio 145 v; p. 30: Borg. Lat. 425 folio 38 v; p. 32: Vat. Lat. 3781 folio 37 v; p. 33: Ottob. Lat. 743 folio 124 r; p. 35: Urb. Lat. 430 folio 10 v; p. 36: Urb. Lat. 273 folio 3 v; p. 37: Urb. Lat. 112 folio 527 v; p. 38: Borg. 183 folio 23 r; p. 39: Chigi CVIII 234 folio 250 r; p. 42: Chigi CVII 205 folio 3 r; pp. 44, 45: Chigi CVIII 234 folio 3 v—4 r; p. 47: Chigi CIV 109 folio 2 r; pp. 48, 49: Vat. Lat. 3769 folio 27 v; p. 50: Chigi CVIII 234 folio 250 r; p. 53: Urb. Lat. 1 folio 201 r; pp. 54, 55: Urb. Lat. 2 folio 31 v; p. 57: Vat. Lat. 3781 folio 43 r; p. 59: Vat. Lat. 3781 folio 40 v; p. 61: Barb. Lat. 613 folio 514 r; pp. 62, 63, 65: Capponi 218 folio 84 r; p. 67: Vat. Lat. 3770 folio 171 v; p. 68: Barb. Lat. 487 folio 49 v; p. 71: Urb. Lat. 2 folio 239 r; p. 73: Capponi 218 folio 87 v; p. 77: Chigi CVII 205 folio 62 r; p. 79: Barb. Lat. 487 folio 47 r; p. 80, back cover: Urb. Lat. 185 folio 68 r.